HAPPINESS HAVEN

Two Talks on Blessedness and

Christ's Way to It

by

Amos R. Wells

First Fruits Press
Wilmore, Kentucky
c2015

Happiness haven : two talks on blessedness and Christ's way to it, by Amos R. Wells.

First Fruits Press, ©2015
Previously published: Boston and Chicago: United Society of Christian Endeavor, ©1912.

ISBN: 9781621714279 (print), 9781621714286 (digital)

Digital version at http://place.asburyseminary.edu/christianendeavorbooks/12/

For all other uses, contact:

First Fruits Press
B.L. Fisher Library
Asbury Theological Seminary
204 N. Lexington Ave.
Wilmore, KY 40390
http://place.asburyseminary.edu/firstfruits

Wells, Amos R. (Amos Russel), 1862-1933.
   Happiness haven : two talks on blessedness and Christ's way to it / by Amos R. Wells.
   80 pages ; 21 cm.
   Wilmore, Ky. : First Fruits Press, ©2015.
   Reprint. Previously published: Boston : United Society of Christian Endeavor, ©1912.
   ISBN: 9781621714279 (pbk.)
   1. Joy. I. Title.
BJ1481 .W5 2015

Cover design by Jonathan Ramsay

asburyseminary.edu
800.2ASBURY
204 North Lexington Avenue
Wilmore, Kentucky 40390

First Fruits
THE ACADEMIC OPEN PRESS OF ASBURY SEMINARY

First Fruits Press
The Academic Open Press of Asbury Theological Seminary
204 N. Lexington Ave., Wilmore, KY 40390
859-858-2236
first.fruits@asburyseminary.edu
asbury.to/firstfruits

HAPPINESS HAVEN

HAPPINESS HAVEN

Two Talks on Blessedness and Christ's Way to It

By AMOS R. WELLS

BOSTON AND CHICAGO
UNITED SOCIETY OF CHRISTIAN ENDEAVOR

Contents

Page

CHRIST'S COMMAND THAT IS
    OFTENEST BROKEN 7

THE BEATITUDES TO-DAY 29

Christ's Command That Is Oftenest Broken

I.

Our Sinful Worries

OUR Lord did not utter many commands. From His gracious mouth proceeded many invitations, many exhortations, many encouragements, many warnings, but few decrees.

The orders that He did issue, however, though they were simple, were so profound and comprehensive that obedience is not at all easy. We break His commandments many times every day, because they relate to every day, and enter our minutest acts.

If you were asked which of Christ's commands is most frequently broken, what would you say?

Some of you might point out the all-inclusive behest, "Be ye perfect, even as your Father in heaven is perfect." But this commandment in the original is not so impossible as it necessarily appears in our English translation; it is the imperative mood in the future tense, which we have not in our language. It commands us to be perfect, but in the good time to come as

[7]

the result of our constant struggle toward perfection here.

Christ uttered other vast commands, such as "Follow me," "Let not thy left hand know what thy right hand doeth," "Love your enemies," "Give to him that asketh thee," "Judge not," "Let your light so shine before men that they may glorify your Father in heaven." All of these reach to the depths of character and to the heights of action. Every one of them is often broken, in thought and in deed.

But of all our Lord's commandments I think the one most frequently and most openly and most inexcusably transgressed is one that is perhaps most often on our lips, one that is very dear to us, one that we do not recognize as a command at all. It is the beautiful words that open the favorite chapter of all the Bible, the fourteenth of John: "Let not your heart be troubled."

We take this as a prophecy of peace: "Your heart will not be troubled."

We take it as a promise of help: "I will remove your trouble from you."

We take it as a mother's sympathetic crooning: "There! There! Don't worry! It'll all come out right."

Undoubtedly all of these thoughts are in the saying, but incidentally and as consequences. In the main, however, when Christ said, "Let not your heart be troubled," He

was uttering a commandment as strict, if
not as stern, as any in the Decalogue. It
is a summons to action, and not to peace;
to struggle against our worries and not ac-
quiescence in them. It does not so much
promise relief as bid us take it. It is not
a comfort to be accepted or rejected, but a
command to be broken or kept. It is at
the peril of our souls that we let our hearts
be troubled.

And yet who is there that does not
worry? And who, even of saintly Christians, counts his worry a deadly sin?

We worry as children, as youth, as ma-
ture men and women, and we worry ourselves into the grave.

We worry over broken dishes and broken
plans and broken hearts.

We worry over torn dresses and severed
friendships.

We worry for fear the bread will not
rise, and for fear we shall lose our posi-
tions. We worry over a sneering word,
over a stumbling speech, over a bad debt,
and over a lost thimble.

We open our eyes upon worries in the
morning, and stare at them in the dark at
night.

We do not fight our worries: we coddle
them. We are rather proud of them, as
proving our discernment. A mind of unfailing serenity, we think, must be a shal-
low mind, and a heedless one.

And there, confronting us in all our fretting, is that masterful command, "Let not your heart—*let* not your heart—LET not your heart be troubled."

Surely this is the commandment that is most frequently broken.

II.

The Body Cure for Trouble

HOW are we to keep it? How are we to prevent our hearts from being troubled? How are we to cure our worries?

The world has four cures, each of them zealously urged by tireless advocates. The first is what I will call the body cure. "Keep in good health," say the believers in this cure, "and you will keep in good heart." This is the *mens sana in corpore sano*. According to this theory, if you are healthy, you will be happy.

And there is much reason back of these claims. Many of our worries are only the mental shadows of undigested puddings. Many of our heartaches have no better origin than headaches. Bad blood is quite likely to break out in bad temper. Flabby muscles have more than a remote connection with flabby will. When the bodily processes move briskly, the mental processes are quite certain not to lag. "The Anatomy of Melancholy" that old Richard Burton wrote about is closely bound up with the anatomy of our bones and the organs they support.

[11]

Therefore the first and most obvious step
along the pathway of obedience to our Saviour's command, "Let not your heart be
troubled," is not to let our bodies be un-
healthy. If, as is undeniably the case, you
can wash off most of your worries by a
plunge in the ocean, or leave them by the
roadside in the course of a brisk walk, or
lose them beyond recovery in the flood of
a sound sleep, then to refrain from the
swim, the walk, the sleep, is to sin against
this commandment of Christ. If dyspepsia
means the blues, and it does mean them,
the deepest indigo, then to be careless of
our eating and our digestion is deliberately
to let our hearts be troubled.

There ought to be no question about it,
in this year of our Lord. Dumb-bells and
Indian clubs are instruments of grace. Physical stamina is on the road to spiritual
stamina. Sins of the body are as sinful as
sins of the soul. The wanton destruction
of health is to be classed with the destruction of virtue, because it leads to it. Health-
iness and holiness are at root the same English word. To train our bodies so that they
are lithe and swift, strong and accurate,
aglow with vigor and aflame with natural
beauty, is in no slight degree to train our
souls to vigor, to beauty, and to peace.

In no slight degree, and yet not in the
fullest degree. Not only by keeping our
bodies from sickness can we keep our hearts

from troubles. The finest athletes are not always saints—far from it, often. Our days of highest physical delight, our vacation days, are by no means free from depression and anxiety. On the other hand, some of the world's greatest sufferers, such as Robert Louis Stevenson, have been its happiest examples of sunny serenity.

It would seem, therefore, that we must look beyond health for the final cure for worry. Health is a mighty help, but it is no specific. We need more than a good digestion if we are not to let our hearts be troubled.

III.

The Mind Cure for Trouble

THE second of the world's cures for
trouble may be called the mind cure.
It takes many forms, some of them quite
fantastic and absurd. With some it is an
attempt to philosophize trouble out of existence, to deny that sin exists, or disease,
or anything else that can make trouble.
"God is good," these thinkers insist, "and
God is all and in all, and therefore all
things are good and there is no evil. Believe this," they urge; "believe it with all
your mind, refuse to believe anything else,
and you will keep your heart from trouble."

There are others who do not go so far as
to deny the existence of pain and sickness
and sin; they admit that these give quite
substantial and continual proofs of their
existence; that, indeed, if we are not to
believe that they exist we can quite as
well convince ourselves that nothing exists,
not even man, not even God. But they say
that the mind has a vast and well-nigh un-
limited power over the body and also over
itself. They say that, just as a man can
make himself sick by brooding over disease
symptoms, so he can keep himself well by
meditating on what is healthful and cheery.

[14]

They make much of the verse, "As a man thinketh in his heart, so is he," quite oblivious to the fact that that is an altogether wrong translation.

These philosophers exalt the human will. "Will yourself happy," they say, "and you will be happy. These doubts and fears and worries crowd your heart just because you do not drive them out."

They bid us set forth upon each new day with our minds fixed upon purity and strength and peace. They bid us resolve within ourselves that we will not grow angry, or envious, or discouraged, or worried. They bid us make up our minds what sort of person we want to become, and presto! we shall be just that sort of person. That is the mind cure for trouble.

Now I should be the last to deny that this cure is efficacious. There is no worry that may not be doubled and trebled by brooding over it. Indeed, such brooding hatches out dozens of new worries that rapidly grow as big as the parent trouble. There is a curt phrase of current slang: "Forget it!" and that phrase contains a world of sound philosophy.

To a large extent, the mind controls its occupants. Like a first-class hotel, it may refuse to entertain vagrants, guests without baggage, guests of doubtful character. To a large extent, the mind can shift its thoughts from one line to another as readily as a train of cars may be switched. We may, with the exercise of resolution, deliberately exile ideas and feelings that are hurtful, and crowd our minds with the thoughts that are helpful. Since we can do this, it is worse than weak, it is actually sinful, not to do so.

"To a large extent," I say; and yet not wholly. The human mind is powerful, but not omnipotent. Barricade it as we will, sometimes a rush of demons will tear the barriers down. Cleanse it and purify it as we will, there are miasmas that fly upon the winds and spread abroad through the very sunshine.

Even the power of a well-disciplined mind has in it the elements of a dangerous pride, that Satan uses to our destruction. Even the house that is most emptied of devils, emptied, and swept, and garnished, may afford a home for seven worse devils than the first. Whoever has tried to will himself into happiness has found sooner or later that his will is a broken reed. Paul tried it with his matchless mind, and cried at last in despair, "What I would, that do I not; but what I hate, that do I. When I would do good, evil is present with me. O wretched man that I am!"

IV.

The Play Cure for Trouble

THE third of the world's cures for trouble is the play cure.

This is a popular cure, very pleasant to take. The old like it almost as well as the young. It is favored by the learned and the ignorant. It is the basis of a system of moral philosophy of the highest respectability and more than two thousand years old.

We do not often call it play; we prefer the more dignified term, "recreation." The right kind of recreation, we say, is a *re*-creation. It makes us over. It sloughs off what was not in us by original creation, and puts us back into the sweet and pure state of nature. We become like children, and so enter the kingdom of heaven.

Thus the millions seek to bury their troubles in the ponds with a fish-line, or race away from their troubles in an automobile, or dance off their troubles in the ballroom, or crowd out their troubles by the fictitious images of the theatre, or lose their troubles on the links with the golf-ball, or shuffle off their troubles with a pack of cards.

And this cure also has genuine curative

[17]

qualities, if it is rightly used. Most of us worry too much because we play too little. Our bow is always bent, and soon grows stiff and breaks. The razor of our mind is never rested, and soon it ceases to cut.

Play is a tonic. It takes us brightly and decisively out of our gloomy surroundings. It lifts us from the ruts, where we were imprisoned along with our worries. It does not deprive the clouds of their rain and their lightning; but it puts us above them, where we can look down upon their silver lining.

The right kind of recreation stimulates the body or the mind or both. It breaks the current of gloomy thoughts, and enables us to turn them into happier channels. It gets us out amid the freshness and purity of the woods and fields. It forces us into pleasant human associations. It is a powerful ally of both the body cure for trouble and the mind cure for trouble.

And yet with play alone, even play at its best, no one can keep his heart from being troubled. The ancient wise man tried it. "I said in mine heart, Go to now, I will prove thee with mirth, therefore enjoy pleasure; and I withheld not my heart from any joy." But the result of it all was the sad confession, "Vanity of vanities; all is vanity and vexation of spirit."

This has been the conclusion of every disciple of Epicurus, of every one who has

sought peace in pleasure. Recreation for
its own sake does not re-create. Troubles,
whelmed in play, distracted by play,
soothed by play, have a maddening fashion
of reappearing as soon as play is over.
Those whose life is most persistent in the
pursuit of recreation are often the saddest
at heart. Not thus may one prevent his
heart from being troubled.

V.

The Work Cure for Trouble

THE fourth of the world's cures for trouble is the work cure.

This is the cure that is most popular among modern Americans. Careless of the body, impatient of philosophy, preferring to watch while others play, the modern American, in the main, does not rely upon any one of the three remedies we have discussed. But he does believe in work. He is confident that work, if it is only hard enough, will cure every evil and bring about every blessing.

And he is not far from right. At least, activity, well-directed and constant activity, is one of the unfailing springs of health, and happiness, and peace.

Hard work at any honorable task is a glorious remedy for worry. The mind in pursuit of a worth-while result ceases to pursue will-o'-the-wisps or to run panic-stricken from hobgoblins. The back that is carrying any noble burden has no room for an old man of the sea. If at the end of the day you can survey any sound achievement, whether it be a corn-field ploughed, or a dress made, or a fence built, or some

[20]

loaves of bread baked, or a beautiful poem written, or a beautiful picture painted, you cannot look upon that sight with clouded eyes and a heavy heart.

If you would not let your heart be troubled, do not let your hands be idle. The mischief that Satan finds for idle hands is very often the setting up of men of straw to worry over. How that delights the devil!

Idle hands are digging pitfalls. Idle minds are studying ruin. Do you remember what the nobleman said in the parable as he gave the pounds to his servants? His command was, "Occupy till I come." That is our Lord's command to all His servants, "Occupy till I come again." Occupation is a better medicine than laughter. Occupation is a better drill than a gymnasium. Occupation is a better school than a college. Occupation is itself a recreation.

If you have learned to fill your days, to their ultimate minute, with useful labors for hand and brain, you will be very likely at the same time to fill them with happiness and peace.

But again I must qualify; I must say "very likely"; I cannot say "certainly."

For industry does not always mean serenity. Lord Avebury wrote two inspiring essays: one on "The Happiness of Duty" and the other on "The Duty of Happi-

ness"; but he could not in the same way
couple happiness and work.

At present, for example, the laboring
classes, so called, those whose industry is
most incessant, those whose labors produce
the most patent and substantial results,
are the most restless, dissatisfied, and un-
happy portion of humanity, and with very
good reason.

Indeed, it is very remarkable to note the
absence of exhortations to industry from
the recorded words of our Saviour.   He
was a carpenter, and He knew from His
human experience the spiritual value of
toil, yet no Beatitude is based upon labor,
and the happiness that He prescribes for
us and commands upon us has quite other
sources and guarantees.

Work is blessed.   Work is happiness-
producing.   Work is one of the highest pre-
rogatives of life.   But work alone will not
prevent our hearts from being troubled.

VI.

The Christ Cure for Trouble

HOW, then, are we to obey Christ's command, not to let our hearts be troubled? How, if health is no impregnable barrier to worry? How, if the mind has no indomitable force against it? How, if pleasure has no victorious lure to trap it? How, if work has no tools to build an enduring palace of joy? What means does Christ offer for the keeping of His own command?

He offers—Himself!

"Let not your heart be troubled"—the whole world knows the words by heart— "Let not your heart be troubled: ye believe in God, believe also in me." That is Christ's prescription for happiness: simply belief in Himself.

But why did He not stop with belief in God? Especially since He Himself was one with God? Why did He add those strange words, "Believe also in me"?

Because belief in God is not the prescription for happiness; the prescription is belief in Christ.

The ancient Hebrews believed in God, and shuddered before His awful sanctuary, bowed their heads while the high priest

passed behind the mysterious veil, and
through most of their history ran away
from Him to the more attractive gods of
the heathen.

Even to-day there are many who believe
in God, but only as the stern embodiment
of fate, slaughtering thousands with an
earthquake shock, heaping just and unjust
in common graves, of twenty seeds bringing but one to bear, of twenty noble lives
bringing but one to happy fruition.

Yes, even the devils believe—and trem-
ble.

Belief in God will not make one happy,
will not keep one's heart from being troubled. The question must go deeper than
that: "What kind of God do you believe
in?"

Believe in the Christ God! That is the
secret of an untroubled life, and the only
secret.

Believe in the God that enters humanity,
that makes a little child the guardian of
His kingdom, that sleeps in a manger and
toils in a carpenter-shop.

Believe in the God that walks our dusty
ways, that endures our homelessness, that
buffets our storms by land and sea.

Believe in the God that lays hands upon
the leper, that calms the lunatic, that summons the dear one back from the grave.

Believe in the God that whips rascals,
that weeps over sinning municipalities,

that confronts false councillors with silent condemnation.

Believe in the God that has His Gethsemanes and His Calvaries as well as His mounts of transfiguration and ascension.

You may already believe in God. You see Him on Mount Olympus, when now and then the parting clouds give glimpses of Him. He is feasting in an inaccessible heaven, or He is hurling thunderbolts at an offending earth. You believe in God, but you do not believe in the infinite Father, the universal Lover, the omnipotent and perfect Friend. And so your heart is troubled, and with that belief you must let it remain troubled.

Do not stop there. "Ye believe in God, believe also in me." Believe in the God whom the world could never have guessed without Christ. Believe in the God who throws His arm around you, who takes your hand in His. And, believing with all your heart, your heart will no more be troubled.

VII.

An Untroubled Life

HOW significant it is that Christ could say, "Ye believe in God, believe also in me," and even those that do not believe in Him receive the saying with respect! Christ is not ridiculed for egotism or condemned for blasphemy. Even to infidels it seems the natural thing for Him to say. That seeming is one of the proofs of the assertion.

But a mightier, an overwhelming proof is the experience of the troubled heart itself. It is not an experience difficult to obtain, nor a proof hard to demonstrate.

If it were a matter of health, the tiniest microbe might confuse it. If it were a matter of philosophy, the least flaw in a syllogism would refute it. If it were a matter of recreation, a trifling touch of degeneration would annul it. If it were a matter of toil, it would be defeated by weariness or failure. But since it is only the soul's attitude, only a reaching out toward Christ, only the yielding of self that He may take possession, the proof depends upon Him and not upon ourselves, and we are only to receive and enjoy.

And immediately, after we have entered

this belief in Christ, all the agencies through which we have been vainly seeking relief from trouble receive new efficacy from Him, and gain a new significance.

Our body is recognized now as the temple of His indwelling. We have this powerful motive to keep it pure and strong. In the inspiring task we have the help of the new occupant. Our bodies are transformed by the renewing of our minds. Sickness is conquered by His presence. The seeds of disease are rendered innocuous. Even in physical weakness we discover a spiritual strength. The entire material foundation of life becomes vital, glowing, happiness-producing as soon as it is thus associated with the One who created it.

Our mind becomes the mind of Christ, when we thus receive the Saviour. What a joy, not to think God's thoughts after Him, but to think them with Him! It has become easy to think the trustful thoughts that are confidence, the quiet thoughts that are serenity. It has become an instinct to will our way into happiness, because it is now God who works in us to will and to do of His good pleasure.

Our play for the first time becomes genuine re-creation when thus associated with the Lord of creation. We have now in His inward voice the unfailing test of helpful or harmful sports. We have now the lofty purpose and Presence that dignify the most hilarious amusement. We have never before known what recreation is.

And our work! How glorious it grows, when Christ enters into it! What an incentive, to achieve results with Him! What an inspiration is the sense of His comradeship in our toil! Failure at once becomes impossible to us forevermore. Though the world may never call us successful, our goal is won, for it is the loving presence of Christ. The results of our work together are His concern. We know that they will come, in His good time, and we are happy in His will and way.

Yes, whatever may be our surroundings or our fortune, we are happy in His will and way. We no longer need the command, "Let not your heart be troubled." Our troubles are a half-obliterated memory. They are like the dream of another world, a different and sad existence. We have entered the kingdom of heaven, which is righteousness and peace and joy in Christ's Holy Spirit. In seeking to fulfil His command we have fulfilled His prophecy. His joy is in us, and our joy is fulfilled.

Ah, brothers and sisters, it is all so easy and simple. It hardly needs the repeated telling, but for our repeated neglect and forgetfulness. God forgive us that so often we let our hearts be troubled. Christ help us to keep this commandment that is oftenest broken.

The Beatitudes To-day

I.

Happiness, or Blessedness?

IN our commonly used translations the Beatitudes begin with "Blessed"; the true thought is rather, "Happy."

All men want to be happy; few men want to be blessed.

Blessedness is the happiness of angels, happiness is the bliss of men; and few men want to be angels—at least, not right away.

Blessedness is happiness glorified, spiritualized, enriched with wisdom and grace.

The Greek word translated "blessed" is the ordinary word for "happy." Christ put the blessedness into it. Christ lifted it up into spiritual places. This is only one of many words that Christianity has exalted. "Christian" itself is another.

But to read this ennobled word into the fifth chapter of Matthew is an anachronism. Indeed, it is a confusing of the effect with the cause, for the fifth chapter of Matthew was the chief cause of the transformation.

More than that, the translation, "Blessed," takes away much of the point of Christ's words. For our Lord took men where He

found them, though He never left them
there. He found them seeking happiness,
and He left them seeking blessedness. But
His first words were always of the happiness they sought, and not of the blessedness
He would have them seek. Not until He
had obtained literal water did He point out
the Water of life. Not until He had dis-
tributed literal bread did He disclose the
Bread of life. Paul followed the same
method in Athens when he began with the
gods the Greeks worshipped ignorantly, and
ended by leading them to the Unknown
God.

In effect, the Beatitudes say this: "You
want to be happy. I do not blame you. Indeed, I will help you. You need help, for
you are travelling the wrong road. You
will never reach happiness the way you are
going, but by a way that runs quite opposite. Turn about, follow me, and yours
will be the happiness for which you long."

The Beatitudes are Christ's guide-book
to happiness. The road is so different from
the one ordinarily travelled that we have
given a new name to its destination, calling
it blessedness. But that confuses the issue
between Christ and worldlings. They want
to be happy, and Christ says, "I alone can
make you so." "Blessedness" implies making others happy, and worldlings are not
eager to do that. It implies holiness of
character, and worldlings do not care for

that. What they want is just to be happy.
"Very well," said Christ, "I know the only
way." Therefore He placed the Beatitudes
at the front of His message to the world.

And so I think it would be impossible
to exaggerate the importance of insisting
upon this use of "happy" rather than
"blessed" in the Beatitudes. The entire
appeal of Christianity and method of its
presentation are involved in this.

Say to any worldling that a holy bliss is
experienced by mourners, the meek, the
pure in heart, the persecuted, and he will
not dispute you, neither will he be inter-
ested; he is not in pursuit of a holy bliss.
He is in pursuit of a good time, and whatever promises a good time will interest
him. Christ in the Beatitudes promises a
good time.

This is not to say that there is not something vastly better than a good time. This
is not to place happiness on a level with
blessedness. This is not to adopt the low
ideals of the world.

It is only to begin where Christ began,
that we may end where Christ ended. He
did not speak out of the opening heaven
and bid men fly up thither. He came down
where men were. He did not even on earth
present Himself as a shining angel, purity
and power gleaming from a countenance of
dazzling beauty, and borne upon wings
over the dusty roads of Palestine. He

came as a man, a poor man, a working
man, the lowliest of the lowly. He set
Himself alongside the humblest human lot.
"This is what the Father is always doing,"
He said; and that is the sum of His gos-
pel.

Would it not have been strange, then,
thus taking life as He found it, and thus
entering into it simply and brotherly, if
He had begun by ministering to needs that
men did not feel, and offering joys that
men did not desire? Why, it would have
been at variance with His entire life and
character.

No. Men want to be rich; Christ was
poor, yet making many rich. Men want to
be powerful. "All power," said Christ, "is
given to me, and through me to my disciples." Men want above all things to be
happy, and Christ's first word to them is
of this supreme desire.

Let us imitate our Saviour in this way
of approaching people. There is too much
giving, not of what men long for, but of
what we think they ought to long for. The
merchant's success is based upon a knowledge of human nature; so is the politician's; so is the Christian worker's. We
are to go forth into the highways and
hedges of human nature and there invite
our brothers to the feast. We shall never
get them by sending gilt-edged invitations
through the mail.

II.

Happy Are the Poor
Happy Are the Rich

"HAPPY are the poor," wrote Luke, in his report of the Sermon on the Mount. "Happy are the poor *in spirit*," wrote Matthew, in his report.

Which did Christ say? or did He say both? and in that case was the second a commentary on the first, "Happy are the poor when they are also poor in spirit"?

We must remember that Christ was preaching to an impoverished people, almost an enslaved people, and that most of His followers were sunk in the depths of literal poverty. For that day, when practically all wealth was wicked, and almost all saints were poor, the dangers of wealth and the spiritual advantages of poverty needed to be emphasized, and Christ emphasized them. More easily, He said, can a camel squeeze himself through a needle's eye than a rich man squeeze into the Kingdom of God. He bade the rich young ruler sell all that he had and give the proceeds away. He painted the doom of Dives and the eternal joy of Lazarus. "Woe unto you that are rich," He cried. In His par-

[33]

able He pictured the deceitfulness of riches
as choking the good seed in human hearts.
Poor Himself, homeless and penniless and
often lacking bread, He opened His cata-
logue of the happy with poor folks.

Now this is precisely opposed to the theory and practice of the world, and to the
practice if not the theory of most Christians.

"Happy are the rich," we cry, even while
we piously ejaculate, "Blessed are the
poor." We advocate missions and long for
automobiles. We recommend self-denial
and inquire the price of sealskins. We
sing, "Thou, O Christ, art all I want,"
when an honest list of our wants would
fill the hymn-book. We confess that the
love of money is a root of all kinds of evil,
and we try to uproot it and fill our bins
with it.

Let us be done with such hypocrisy. Let
us admit that we want to be rich, and that
not merely, as we so often unctuously say,
for the good we could do to others with
the money, but also for the good, the very
pleasant good, we could do to ourselves.

And in this we are entirely Christian.
For if poverty is the ideal life, why did
Christ recommend the rich young ruler to
give his possessions to the poor? Why not
leave the poor in their superior state? Why
alleviate their happiness? Why comfort
their bliss?

The earth is the Lord's, and the fulness thereof; the Lord's, and not the devil's; the earth, and not merely heaven; the Lord's, and also His children's. All things are ours, since we are Christ's, and Christ is God's; all things, things present as well as things to come.

Christ came eating and drinking. He visited rich men's homes, and was buried in a rich man's grave. He praised John the Baptist, man of the locusts and wild honey, but said that the least of His own Kingdom was greater than John. The monks and nuns, with their vows of perpetual poverty, are in that the poorest representatives of our Lord.

For poverty is debasing. It cramps body and stupefies the mind and benumbs the soul. Poverty is the handmaid of ignorance, the parent of debauchery, the brother of despair. Poverty stretches the human spirit upon the rack of toil. It narrows experience. It lowers taste. It sears the soul. Poverty is the primal curse of Eden, poverty and not labor.

Wealth, on the other hand, is a great blessing. It affords leisure, the nutriment of character. It gives its possessor the chance for friendship, for knowledge, for culture. Wealth is art, and music, and books, and travel. Wealth means development, and influence. To affect a scorn of wealth is insanely to scorn these blessings.

"Happy are ye," Christ said to His poor, "not because of your poverty, but in spite of it; because ye are poor also in spirit, repentant, humble, and trusting, and therefore are heirs of my Kingdom." He would say the same to-day to all the poor that are poor in spirit, to all the poor that belong to His Kingdom.

But ah, with what emphasis would Christ say to-day: "Happy are the rich who are also poor in spirit, happy are the rich who are eager and active to enrich the world! Happy are the rich who are spending themselves to abolish poverty!"

For poverty is the sin of the modern rich. In a land like ours, with its enormous natural advantages and its free institutions, and in a time like ours, when science and invention have laid the natural forces at our feet, the prevalence of poverty is more than a misfortune, it is a disgrace.

If our land were Christian, there would be no poverty. There would be degrees of wealth, but no suffering from want, and no fear of want.

Christ's own teachings have lifted the world into a region where some of them are no longer literally to be followed. To-day Christ would hardly bid the rich man to sell all he has and give to the poor; but He would surely bid the rich man to use all he has for the abolishing of poverty.

There is coming a time when the Beatitude of the first century, "Happy are the poor," will coalesce with the Beatitude of the twentieth century, "Happy are the rich"; for the poor will be no longer with us. In that day all will toil, and all will enjoy leisure. If wealth is an excess of riches above others, there will be no wealth, for greed will have lost its golden mask, and will be seen in its own hideous aspect.

That will be the kingdom of heaven. Remember, it is to come on earth. It is not a kingdom of beggars and paupers, any more than it is a kingdom of misers and thieves. Happy will be the poor when they enter into it. Happy will be the rich when they make it possible. Happy will be the poor in spirit, whether impoverished or opulent, who, dethroning pride and greed, in the brother-love which our Saviour taught and exemplified transform this world into one great family, where the good of one is the good of all, on earth as it is in heaven. The happiness of poverty is a temporary happiness, made possible and certain by the conquering presence of Christ in the poverty. The happiness of wealth is the permanent happiness, to be enjoyed on earth by Christ's rich men who are laboring with Christ to make all men rich, and to be enjoyed by all in the kingdom of heaven, when riches will be the lot of all Christ's happy followers.

III.

Happy Are the Mourners
Happy Are the Laughers

"BLESSED are they that mourn"! Of all Christ's paradoxes none is more paradoxical than this. It is as if He had said, "Happy are the sad."

In harmony with the saying, or its imagined import, Christ is pictured in prophecy as a man of sorrows, acquainted with grief. He is shown in the Gospels as weeping, at the grave of Lazarus, on the hill overlooking Jerusalem; but never as laughing. He is imaged by the great artists as pallid with long vigils and burdened with a weight of anguish.

Still further in harmony with the saying uncounted numbers of Christ's followers have immured themselves in gravelike cells, have worn only the black garb of the mourner, and have afflicted themselves with fastings, flagellations, and tortures almost unendurable. By the path of sorrow, the road to the tomb, they have expected to reach the summit of bliss.

To-day, in absolute revolt from all this, multitudes are surging to the other extreme, and are seeking happiness in a de-

[38]

nial of sorrow. They are training their eyes to be tearless. They are exercising their souls in the art of oblivion. They are stoutly saying to Sin, "I know you not," and to Pain, "You are only a ghost," and to all Suffering, "You are emptiness and nothing."

"Don't worry" has become to many the sum of the law, the one commandment. "Laugh at grief," their philosophy bids, "and it will break as a bubble." "All is mental," these idealists urge, "and all is to be controlled if the mind is controlled." Therefore they are surrounding themselves with cheerfulness, with bright paper on the walls, and bright lights in the ceilings, and with flowers and music and smiling pictures and youthful voices.

How empty and unworthy would this gay teaching appear to the Galilean! as trivial as the monkish mourning, and both of them utterly untrue to Him!

For when Christ said, "Happy are the weepers," He did not exalt sorrow into a virtue, but he did acknowledge the necessity of sorrow. He "saw life steadily, and saw it whole." When He drove the hired mourners out of the house of Jaïrus, it was because they were hired, not because they were mourners. When He said, "The damsel is not dead, but sleeping," it was only as we call our graveyards "cemeteries," that is, "sleeping-grounds." The lovely,

tender metaphor did not deny death, any
more than in the case of Lazarus, when He
said, "Our friend Lazarus sleepeth," but
immediately added plainly, "He is dead."
Our Redeemer did not deny sin; He con-
stantly spoke of sinners as lost men. He
did not deny sorrow, or count it a means
of grace, but prayed that the cup of His
sufferings might pass from Him.

But on the other hand, the Saviour exalted happiness. Here at the outset of His
ministry He is giving prescriptions for it.
At the close of His ministry He said,
"These things have I spoken unto you,
that my joy might remain in you, and that
your joy might be full"—His joy, only an
hour before Gethsemane!

True, it is not recorded that Jesus
laughed; but what laughter does the Bible
record? In the Old Testament, only the
incredulous laughter of Abraham and Sa-
rah, mocking at the Lord's promise; the
scornful laughter of the Israelites when
Hezekiah proclaimed his passover; the sar-
castic laughter of Sanballat and his friends
when Nehemiah began to build the wall;
in the New Testament, only the sneering
laughter of the hired mourners in the house
of Jaïrus when Jesus said, "The damsel is
not dead, but sleepeth." There is not in
all the Bible a single record of a genuine
laugh.

Indeed, has not Christianity alone

brought laughter to men's lives? India,
the most idolatrous of lands, is the saddest
of lands. China, that vast domain, has no
room for a smile. Africa is the continent
of haunting fear. But the Christian lands,
with all their misery and sin, are neverthe-
less vibrant with at least beginnings of
laughter.

Luke reports the Beatitude thus : "Happy
are you that weep now, for you shall
laugh." Did He merely look forward to
the happy land from which He came, the
land where God would wipe away all tears
from all eyes? No; He looked forward
also in glad assurance to the establishment
of His Kingdom on earth, that kingdom
which is not only righteousness and peace
but also joy. In spite of their mourning
now, they should laugh in the happy time
to come. The happiness of the mourner is
to be swallowed up in the happiness of the
laugher.

Therefore let us not reproach ourselves
if we find it impossible for us to rejoice by
the death-beds of our dear ones, if the hot
tears will persist in coming, and the heart
goes heavy all the day long. Our Christ
is sorrowing with us. He is not pretending lightly that it is nothing. He is not
pressing to our tear-wet cheeks a comic
mask. He is not trying to force us into
an artificial happiness.

But He is saying, with all the sympathy

of infinite love and with all the confidence of infinite knowledge: "Laughter is coming back some day. There are smiles behind the tears. There are compensations to balance all sorrows. Not all things are good, but all things work together for good, all things combine into a happy solution." This is the Beatitude, to know this.

Over against it our Master uttered a warning: "Woe unto you that laugh now," He said sternly, "for you shall mourn and weep." This laughter that has woe in it is the only kind that the Bible records. It is the empty laugh of infidelity, the laugh of selfishness and scorn. The world is full of it to this very day. It floats back from the automobile rushing away from the mangled form of a little child. It rings from the palaces built upon child labor and the oppression of the poor. It sounds from the high places of the earth, filled too often with men that make a mock of God. And He that sitteth in the heavens shall laugh.

But still, as year adds to year its amplifying wisdom and fructifying grace, the Christian laugh, with joy in it and not woe, is growing in the earth. With the strengthening of human bodies, the enfranchising of human minds, the purifying of society, the deepening of brotherhood, with above all the better obeying of Christ, we are learning to laugh as He laughed. Thus year by year we are approaching the time when the sad, necessary Beatitude of Palestine, "Blessed are the mourners," shall be absorbed and lost in the Beatitude of the New Jerusalem, "Blessed are they that laugh."

"Happy are the mourners," said Christ, "because I am with them, adding my tears to theirs, and pointing forward to the sure time when the world's Beatitude of laughter shall be realized in the lives of all my children."

IV.

Happy Are the Meek
Happy Are the Hustlers

NO Christian virtue so lacks appreciation as meekness. About no other are we so hypocritical. With our mouths we say, "Blessed are the meek, for they shall inherit the earth." By our acts and our instinctive admirations we too often say, "Happy are the hustlers, who want the whole earth, and get it."

By the meek Jesus meant the gentle, and so Dr. Moffat translates the word. He meant the retiring, kindly, yielding, modest folks, who do not resent harshnesses, who turn the other cheek to a second blow, who go the second mile, who give their coats to the thieves of their vests. These are the workers that can be imposed upon, that are willing to do more than their share. They are always on the hard committees, but never as chairmen, nor are their names printed in the programmes of the annual meeting. They sign subscription lists, "A Friend." They take the lowest seats at the table, and stay there. It is of them that the sneer is current, "They do not dare to say that their souls are their own."

[44]

To speak of such as these as inheriting the earth seems to an honest modern no less than laughable. "The world for the hustlers!" we virtually if not virtuously cry. Our entire system of business competition is built upon it. Our political methods are based upon it. Society, in its most vaunted aspects, is thus founded. The motto is even to be read occasionally over college entrances, and it is inscribed in Gothic letters above the portals of perhaps three metropolitan churches.

The valued man of 1912 is the man who advertises successfully. He is the man who is "on his job" "with both feet" and all the time. He "delivers the goods," and chiefly to his own back door. He "gets there"; and if any one else was there before him, he establishes a vacancy just before he arrives.

Meekness, gentleness, considerateness, self-concealment, are not virtues to A. D. 1912, whatever they may have been in A. D. 30. A chip on the shoulder is our modern epaulet. Most of us live at No. 1 High Street. Most of us worship success without a preliminary analysis. All of us dislike selfishness, but we do not despise it, unless it fails. If it succeeds, we do not call it selfishness, we call it enterprise.

Now I do not believe that so many Christians would instinctively take this attitude toward the hustlers if there were not some-

thing Christian in hustling. Indeed, I am
prepared to find something essentially
Christian in everything that real Christians honestly admire. I am for discover-
ing what it is, and for ceasing our hypocrisy in pretending to admire the opposite.

And in studying the character and life
of Jesus Christ I find the point of contact
between the meek and the hustlers, the perfect reconciliation of the modern and the
ancient Beatitudes.

To be sure, Jesus was the meekest of
men. When his cruel and bigoted fellow
townsmen would throw Him over the cliff
at Nazareth He did not smite them with
lightning, He merely passed through the
mob and quietly went His way. When,
after the feeding of the five thousand, His
exultant followers wanted to make Him a
king, He hid Himself near Tyre. When
Peter smote Malchus in His defence, He
healed the wound and bade the headstrong
disciple put up His sword. When slander
and bigotry and hatred were doing their
worst, before the Sanhedrim and Herod
and Pilate, as a lamb before its shearers is
dumb, so He opened not His mouth. Yes,
even on the cross, even in the first wild
rush of physical torture, He cried: "Father, forgive them! They know not what
they do."

But all this meekness was regarding
Himself. Regarding His Father's business,

regarding the kingdom of heaven, Jesus
was no longer a Lamb, He was the Lion of
Judah. Nor was it only in the repeated
cleansing of the Temple with literal lash
and the severer sting of righteous wrath.
Nor was it merely in His fierce condemnation of the "scribes, Pharisees, hypocrites,"
the devourers of widows' houses, the bind-
ers of heavy burdens. Nor was it only in
the rebuke of demons and the imperious
quieting of the tempest.

Not the most hustling broker on Wall
Street was a more strenuous worker than
Jesus Christ. Not the most consummate
advertiser of this advertising age can so
effectively commend goods as Jesus could.
In the meeting and mastering of competition, in thoroughness of application, in
tireless persistency, in unfaltering zeal, in
sureness of touch, in accuracy of vision,
and in sleepless energy, our Lord has no
equal among the successful men even of
America.

He enjoyed His work; it was His meat
and drink. He never had a thought apart
from it. His miracles advertised it as no
enterprise before or since has been advertised. His marvellous words commended
it to the millions as nothing else has ever
been commended. He set on foot the world's
vastest organization, and He did it with
the smallest resources in money, men, and
worldly power. For enterprise, for push,

for industry, and for success, no promoter
the world has ever known, no hustler of the
hustlers, no strenuous of the strenuous, is
to be compared with the divine Founder of
our religion.

And He is inheriting the earth. And
His are inheriting the earth. The selfish
hustlers may grab it, but the meek Naza-
rene seizes it out of their grasp. Perfect
meekness for one's self, combined with the
most impetuous ardor for God and man, always have triumphed, and always will.

Happy indeed are the hustlers who are
thus meek and unselfish; happy indeed are
the meek who are thus aggressive. By
His flaming example our Lord thus added
a corollary to His third Beatitude. Thus
He commended His religion to the most
energetic and manly. Thus He preserves
their strength from greed and brutality.
Thus to meekness He adds might and to
might He adds meekness, the manly and
the womanly elements of the perfect Christian.

V.

Happy Are the Hungry
Happy Are the Satisfied

THE fourth Beatitude, like the first, is spiritualized in Matthew's report of the sermon. He says, "Blessed are they that hunger and thirst after righteousness, for they shall be filled." Luke leaves it on the material plane: "Blessed are ye that hunger now, for ye shall be filled." We may well believe that Jesus gave utterance to both sayings, the one being a comment upon the other, and that He began with declaring those happy that were suffering, as so many in His audiences always had suffered, with physical hunger.

It is said that the larger part of the earth's population, namely, the majority of the hundred millions of India and China, never, from one year's end to another, know what it means to satisfy their hunger. We, in our land of plenty, have really no conception of this condition. Our physicians make it their chief warning that we shall not overeat, and devise for us elaborate systems of thorough mastication, that we may avoid that temptation. It is no temptation to the average Oriental.

"Happy are the hungry"—those words

[49]

of Christ were indeed news to His hearers.
To our gorged and gormandizing civilization they are somewhat obvious. "Never
rise from the table quite satisfied," we are
advised. "Never eat till you are hungry."
the wise men tell us. And with many the
chief object of exercise is to get up an ap-
petite. Our wealthy Western world is in
the condition of the millionaire, who looks
with envious eyes at his office-boy, munch-
ing with a relish his pie and doughnuts out
of a tin pail.

Yes, and as to the higher aspects of life
we Westerners are in the same predica-
ment. Our life has become so complex,
we are so rich in interests and excitements,
that a terrible ennui has settled upon us
like a pall. We hear so many delightful
speakers that not even Webster or Glad-
stone could move us to enthusiasm. We
see so many books that the wittiest and
wisest pages arouse in us no surprise and
create only a languid pleasure. We have
so many meetings that we have lost the
glow of comradeship. We have heard so
many sermons that we are gospel-hardened.
Our spiritual emotions have been stimu-
lated so often and so powerfully that they
would respond only feebly should Calvary
be enacted before us. "Verily, verily."
we cry, "are those blessed that can hunger,
really hunger, after righteousness"; and
all our churches are filled with longings

for the first blessed ardor of conversion.

But is this what Christ meant when He declared, "Happy are the hungry"? Not in either case. He was neither lauding starvation nor condemning satisfaction. "Ye shall be filled" was His joyful promise. He pictured His kingdom, the kingdom of heaven on earth, as a great feast. He did not regard hunger as anything good, but as something good to get rid of, good to relieve and appease. And this of spiritual desire as well as the starvation of the body.

Lowell was conscious that he was expressing only a half-truth when he wrote:

"Of all the myriad moods of mind
   That through the soul come thronging,
Which one was e'er so dear, so kind,
   So beautiful as Longing?"

There is a stimulus in longing, but, like the growing pains of a child, it is not a token of health. Growth, when healthy and normal, comes without pain.

The theory of most commentators upon this Beatitude seems to be that there can be no appreciation without tantalization. Lovers must quarrel before they can know the full bliss of affection. "Absence makes the heart grow fonder." The sinner alone can value purity and peace. One does not really enjoy fair weather till one has weathered a storm.

According to this false conception of

life we sinning mortals have a satisfaction
denied the angels themselves, in that we
have fallen and so can understand the
blessedness of restoration, which, indeed,
you will see solemnly set forth in many a
pious dissertation. Carried to its proper
conclusion, our Lord Himself did not value
heaven until He came to earth, nor realize
the joy of communion with the Father until on Calvary He felt that the Father had
forsaken Him. Carried to a conclusion
still more absurd but entirely logical, according to this theory a satisfaction is possible for men that is denied to the All-holy
God Himself, who created men and their
satisfactions.

No; let us never consider this fourth
Beatitude as placing a premium upon starvation, as glorifying asceticism, as fixing a
halo upon the head of Want. The blessedness of Christ's hungry ones is not in their
hunger, but in spite of it; their happiness
is not now, but is to come when they shall
be filled. Let us not torture ourselves with
the attempt to extract joy out of our present doubts and spiritual perplexities, the
starvation of soul that yearns for comfort,
for peace, for strength, for purity, amid
the unrest and temptations and weaknesses
of this storm-tossed life. We are to be
satisfied, when we awake, in His likeness,
and we are to be happy then, completely
happy, if not before.

Christ came to give life, and to give it
abundantly. Here at last, as the poor old
lady said at the seashore, is something that
there is enough of. There is always enough,
and twelve baskets over, when our Lord
breaks the bread.

Is all this to apologize for the overfilled
gluttons of to-day, the gormandizers of our
expensive hotels, the gormandizers of our
gospel-plethorized churches, the greedy
graspers to mouth and mind who have no
regard for others but only for their own
insatiate maws? Not at all, for such a
life never satisfies. It is a gathering into
a bag with holes. Just as he that eats
more than he digests ends with being able
to eat only gruel, so he that crams into his
mind more spiritual nutriment than he
utilizes in service becomes a spiritual dys-
peptic, unable to retain any soul-food at
all. It is of such gluttons that our Lord
spoke in the Revelation: "Thou sayest, I
am rich, and increased with goods, and
have need of nothing; and knowest not
that thou art wretched, and miserable, and
poor, and blind, and naked."

But the fourth Beatitude asserts the
happiness of real satisfaction, and promises it to us, to take the place of all our
present hungers. "They shall hunger no
more, neither thirst any more," those that
are with Christ in His Kingdom. And as
we are waiting for His Kingdom and

working for it, let us address ourselves, in His strength, to the satisfying of all innocent desires, all worthy aspirations, fully assured that as to earthly parents no pang is so sharp as the hunger of their children, it is even so with our Father in heaven. And so Christ's Beatitude, "Happy are the hungry," is another anticipatory Beatitude, involving as its sure culmination the world's instinctive Beatitude, "Happy are the satisfied," and showing the world the only way thereto.

VI.

Happy Are the Merciful
Happy Are the Masterful

THE fifth Beatitude has for its foundation the groundwork of humility.
"Happy are the merciful, for they shall obtain mercy," implies that they need mercy.
It is parallel to the petition in the Lord's
Prayer, "Forgive us our debts as we forgive our debtors." Others are in debt to
us, but we are even heavier debtors toward
God.

Indeed, no one but the humble is likely
to be merciful. The proud and self-suffi-
cient are pitiless. Needing nothing from
others, they are not moved to give anything
to others. Wrapped in a conceit of righteousness, they condemn the unrighteous
with all severity. Living in what they sup-
pose to be impregnable fortresses, they can
throw stones at all glass houses. They
think they will never need to sing the
prayer,

"The mercy I to others show,
That mercy show to me."

It would seem that this Beatitude, of all
the eight, would meet a cold reception
among the people to whom Christ spoke

[55]

and at the time when He taught. It was nineteen centuries before the Red Cross, and war was pitilessly cruel. It was nineteen centuries before John Howard, and prisons were places of torturing revenges oftener perhaps than of just punishments. The Romans were in the saddle, riding the world with a bridle that drew blood. The Jews, that were ridden over, were as imperious and proud as any Roman. If to a Roman a Jew was a dog, to a Jew a Roman was a pig. An enemy was something to hate, to plot against, to lie in wait for, to leap upon, and to throttle savagely. A tooth for a tooth, an eye for an eye, was the creed even of religion.

To this world of cherished animosities, and to this bitter and unforgetting race, our Saviour dared to preach the opposite doctrine. "Love your enemies," He commanded while they scoffed; "bless them that curse you, do good to them that hate you, and even pray for them that despitefully use you and persecute you." And, while a few, His chosen few, heard and heeded, the great, strong world kept on its pitiless way.

Is it otherwise in this that we call the year of our Lord, 1912? Still, while we repeat in our churches, "Happy are the merciful," do we not assert in our business, political, and social dealings, "Happy are the masterful"?

To be sure, our modern stilettos have plush handles, and are worn beneath our coats. As we have learned in physical warfare to bury our batteries in banks of innocent green turf, as we use smokeless powder, and as we conduct our battles at long range of perhaps ten miles, so we wage our money wars and our social and political wars at long range, and we do not see or know the enemies at whom we so effectively fire. We send poisoned bullets through the post-office and dum-dums by telegraph and bombs by telephone. We spring mines in the court-room. We assassinate through the newspapers. We give death-blows by sight-drafts and foreclosures. It is all very polite, and gentlemanly, and murderous.

A successful business man or politician or a successful society woman, if a church-member, is honored in our churches in proportion to his or her success, without embarrassing scrutiny into the sources and methods of success. An unsuccessful man or woman is looked down upon in our churches, with no investigation of the reasons for failure. Sometimes, perhaps often, the failure is glorious and the success an infamy. Sometimes the failure means Christian mercifulness and the success means devilish masterfulness. Sometimes the man or woman who has been a worldly failure should be given the highest honors of the church, and the successful should be

summarily ejected. Of course there are
many exceptions, and I believe that every
year the conscience of the church is growing more sensitive as the church's intelli-
gence is deepened; but still, in the main,
even among Christians, the debt-collector
is esteemed above the debt-forgiver, the
shrewd bargainer above the man who holds
the losing end, the forceful above the gentle, the masterful above the merciful.

No one was ever so masterful as Jesus
Christ. He said once, "Ye call me Master
and Lord; and ye say well, for so I am."
But do you remember when He said that?
It was after He had washed the disciples'
feet. "If I, then, your Lord and Master,"
said He, "have washed your feet, ye also
ought to wash one another's feet." Then
He added a ninth Beatitude: "If ye know
these things, happy are ye if ye do them."

The few literalists that insist upon the
fulfilment of Christ's command with actual
soap and water may well be emulated by
all Christians, transferring the precept to
the spiritual domain where He Himself
would place it. All around us there are
souls that are weary of the difficult roads,
hot and worn, needing the refreshing bath
of sympathy. All around us are soul
stains, hiding or flaunting, needing, so
sadly needing from men the erasing bath
of forgiveness with which the Son of Man
will supply them at a word of asking. Still

we are in the Upper Room, and still too
often the offices of mercy must wait upon
our pride, while the Master girds Himself
with a towel and takes the basin and ewer.
Some day we shall see that in this He is
most masterful as well as most merciful,
and we shall be eager and proud to kneel
beside Him on the floor. Some day we
shall understand that the world's Beatitude, "Blessed are the masterful," is to be
compassed only by way of Christ's Beatitude, "Blessed are the merciful."

VII.

Happy Are the Pure
Happy Are the Experienced

NO other Beatitude has so touched the imaginations and moved the desires of Christians as the sixth, "Happy are the pure in heart, for they shall see God." Surely He who spoke those words, who made that lovely promise, was pure in heart, tempted in all points as we are tempted and yet without sin. And surely He saw God. No man had seen God at any time, but the only begotten Son, coming from the very bosom of the Father, declared Him to men, told us what He looks like, told us what He says, showed us the manner of His life. And then He assured us that if we keep our hearts pure, we shall have the same imperial privilege.

But what did Christ mean by a pure heart? Through all the Christian ages, and even in the present day, the vast majority of those that have called themselves Christians, especially the Greek and Roman Catholics, have held that purity means withdrawal from the world, and have pictured the monk and the nun as those most likely to see God. They have associated purity with paucity of human intercourse.

The hermits have been the saints. Their priests and their holy men and women must not marry. They must not mingle with the world's buyers and sellers. The church must be a thing apart from the world. The Christ-presence must be shut up in a golden box, inside a golden cross, inside a marble shrine, inside a massive, dark, silent stone temple. Purity has meant isolation, solitude, meagreness of interests, absorption in the central thought of God. All this has been and is much like the monkish systems of the Buddhists, and the monumental aloofnesses of the Hindus. It has its parallel in every natural religion; but is it Christian? Is it what Christ meant by purity of heart?

At any rate, it all runs counter to our natural idea of happiness, which associates joy with experience. With what instinctive admiration we look up to a "man of the world," as we call him grandly; a cosmopolitan man; a man who has travelled widely, has seen strange and remote regions, has witnessed weird customs, has tasted queer foods, has talked with all races of men! Our government, in its placards calling for recruits for the army and navy, appeals to this universal admiration. It shows in gayly colored pictures our soldiers and sailors amid tropic scenes, dazzling the natives with bright uniforms, pitching their tents among palms, or sailing toward the aurora borealis. The small boy gazes with open mouth at the gypsy or the circus-rider, longs to go with him out along the far-stretching roads and into novel experiences, and is eager for the time when he too may explore the world and become a maker of romance.

Similarly the love of adventure is the temptation craftily used by the devil in the beginning of many sins. The boy sees men smoking as if they enjoyed it, and he wants to smoke and see how it feels. He sees men excited with strong drink, and he wants to have the sensation of a reeling and dancing and hilarious world. He reads of dare-devil bandits and prodigiously skilful thieves, and he wants to wear a black mask, and carry a dark lantern and a revolver, and prowl about the streets at midnight.

The hold of the theatre upon men and women is largely this, that it introduces them to endless novelties, it familiarizes them with a wide range of characters and experiences, it lifts them bodily out of the humdrum routine of their uninteresting lives. The romance of the gaming-table for men and of the ballroom for women is the secret of their fascination. And for all, for children and adults, one of the surest defences against sin is occupation, varied and delightful interests, honorable adventures into the domain of the unknown.

Need I remind you how thoroughly our Lord is in evident sympathy with this love of adventure? He, in the supreme and final sense, was a man of the world. We never think of Him as a Jew or even as an Asiatic; He was a cosmopolitan. He became an adventurer. He went forth as a true knight. He had no abiding-place, nowhere to lay His head. Back and forth He wove His wanderings, until perhaps every path in Palestine was familiar with His feet.

And He entered into all experiences. He chose for His disciples a band as motley as Robin Hood's. There was the lofty-minded John and the base-thinking Judas, and the inquiring Thomas, and the systematic Matthew, and the enterprising Philip, and the practical Andrew, and the headstrong Peter. Among His friends were rich and poor, Nicodemus and Bartimæus, Lazarus the rich and Lazarus the beggar. He visited in the homes of Pharisees, and the houses of tax-gatherers. He associated with Mary the holy, and with harlots. He died with thieves and was buried by the Counsellor Joseph. He knew how to meet all men, how to bear Himself in all circumstances, how to participate in all conditions. Is He the man whose ideal of purity would be a pallid monk?

And He sent His disciples forth into all the world. He set His own life as an ex-

ample for theirs. They were to be all
things to all men, as He had been. They,
even more than the Roman historian, were
to count nothing human as foreign to themselves.

And, we may reverently ask, is it not
thus with God Himself? He enters all
hearts, the depraved as well as the holy.
He reads the open book of every mind, the
filthy as well as the noble. He sees every
act, in the darkness as well as at noonday,
acts of cruelty and foulness as well as acts
of self-sacrifice and heroism. In His case,
as in the case of the Messiah, perfect purity co-exists with full-orbed experience.

May it not be thus with the men that
He created? The pure in heart that see
God, must they not be pure in the same
way in which He is pure? It is prophesied
that when we see Him we are to be like
Him. Can we be like Him in more char-
acteristic fashion than this, that we are
able to enter helpfully, sympathetically,
into all lives, into all the experiences of
normal men, and yet remain pure?

Thus it is that the happiness of the
world, resting so largely upon adventurous
experience, is taken up into the happiness
of the Christian. Thus it is that purity
seizes upon romance, and the church yields
no whit in interest to the world. Thus it
is that our varied and fascinating human
affairs not only need not brush the bloom

from our unsullied purity, but they may
even lift us into the large outreaches of the
Infinite One, and show us Him whom really
to see is fulness of life.

VIII.

Happy Are the Peacemakers
Happy Are the Fighters

"PEACE I leave with you,"—these were almost the parting words of Christ to His disciples,—"my peace I give unto you"; but He immediately and significantly added, *"Not as the world giveth, give I unto you."*

In the Beatitude of peace, fittingly the seventh Beatitude, that of the perfect number, did Christ signify the peace of the world, or did He have in mind His peace, which is not such as the world gives? What kind of peace is the aim of the peacemaker whom Christ counts happy, the peacemaker who is to be called a child of God? What kind of peace, on the other hand, had Christ in mind when He said, "Think not that I am come to send peace on earth: I came not to send peace, but a sword"?

It is the tradition that at our Saviour's birth the world was at peace, and the gate of Janus was closed.

"No war or battle's sound
Was heard the world around;
The idle spear and shield were high uphung."

[66]

However that may be, the gate was soon opened again for the passage of troops, and fighting has progressed, with increasing horrors and at increasing cost of money and misery, from that day to this; and well in the van of military prowess, and in the number and ferocity of their wars, have ever been the Christian nations. In this are they Christian? Is this the kind of sword that Christ brought to earth, or do the angels' song at Bethlehem and the seventh Beatitude represent the Christian spirit?

There is no question which the world would choose, if choice is to be made between them. "Happy are the fighters," the world persists in saying, and never, "Happy are the peacemakers." In the world's farce it is always the peacemaker that thrusts his luckless person between the quarrelling clowns, and receives the blows that each intended for the other. After all the generations since Christ lived, after all these millions of sermons and prayers and hymns and gatherings around the communion-table, it is only in our generation that the nations, the Christian nations, have begun to organize for peace. And while Peace waits hopefully at the Hague our armies are swollen to a vaster size than ever before, our navies have become monumental prodigies of force and folly, and every year we waste upon the

possibility of war two-thirds of our na-
tional resources.

Yes, and still further to discount the
Hague, in our relations with one another,
class with class, rich with poor, laborer
with employer, hand worker with head
worker, we are fanning the flames of a war
compared with which all the wars of Napo-
leon were a child's parade.

No wonder, since these warring powers
are raging in the world, that men look for
fighters, and place them at the head of gov-
ernments and corporations and parties and
schools and human enterprises of all kinds.
No wonder that we bow down before the
fighter, and serve him. He seems our only
salvation from chaos, our only hope of success. What avails the thinker, if he will
not fight for his thought? What avails the
loveliest, most winsome character, if it is
immured in a dungeon?

And so all the world, even the hearts on
which the Beatitudes are written, dearly
loves a man of pugnacity. A slugging-
match in a street will draw a bigger crowd
than any gospel singer. A church quarrel
is better advertised than all the sermons
ever preached in that church put together.
The most exalted principles, such as human
freedom, do not receive much attention till
Garrison gets mobbed for them, and Uncle
Tom is beaten, and John Brown is hanged.
What impresses itself upon life is life, and

any cause gets attention as soon as it is made evident that men are putting into it not merely their thoughts and their words and their coins but their blood.

Therefore the best commentary on the seventh Beatitude is Christ's saying, "And I, if I be lifted up from the earth, will draw all men unto me." By that sign, the sign of the cross, He conquered. By that spear which entered his own side, He became the world's peacemaker. "He is our peace," declared Paul, "having slain enmity by the cross."

By way of the cross all the world's peacemakers enter into their happiness. Verily it is not such peace as the world gives or imagines. It means fathers against sons and mothers against daughters and households divided into foes. It means laborers and employers struggling for a just social order. It means war against war. It means battle for the Bible. It means fighting for a free school and a free press. It means clear vision, stout arm, and an unfaltering heart. It means, even yet it means, many a martyrdom.

But—and here is the point of union between the two Beatitudes, "Blessed are the peacemakers" and "Blessed are the fighters"—it means ever the widening of the realm of peace, and that the ground won shall be held immutably. Christ never urged peace at any price. He would not

cry Peace, Peace, where there is no peace.
It is peacemakers that are happy, and not
peace-fakers.   Nothing is settled till it is
settled right.   Christians are peacemakers
because, at whatever cost of pain and struggle and bloodshed, they are engaged in setting things right, in organizing peace upon
the only sure foundation, that of absolute
justice and brother-love.

And they shall be called the children of
God, these peacemakers, these fighters, because it is precisely such work that God is
always doing.   Christ was God's witness,
how greatly He desired to be at peace with
His children.   Calvary was God's witness
that it must be peace through rightness.

IX.

Happy Are the Persecuted
Happy Are the Popular

THE climax of Christ's paradoxical Beatitudes is the last, "Happy are the
persecuted." The condition that He added,
"persecuted for righteousness' sake," or, as
Luke gives it, "for the Son of man's sake,"
does not lessen the strangeness of the saying, since those to whom He was speaking
would not be likely to suffer persecution
from any other cause.

This Beatitude does not seem strange to
us, because we are strangers to persecution. Persecution is a name to us, a hear-
say, a matter of reading. The saying was
quite different to those to whom persecution was a matter of shrinking flesh, of
agonized nerves, and of racked souls. To
the Christian of the first three centuries
this Beatitude meant the torture of his
loved ones with all ingenuities of devilish
cruelty. It meant the abyss of gnawing
poverty. It meant the climax of hate. It
meant absolute loneliness. It meant the
hunted life of a wild beast. It meant burn-
ing disgrace in the eyes of the world's most
honorable men. Whatever sad and terrible
could be packed into a single word was

[71]

crammed into the word, "persecution."
And the persecuted must be regarded
happy! The persecuted were bidden to rejoice! They were commanded to be ex-
ceeding glad! No mere resignation and
grim endurance was to be theirs, no heroism of suffering. There were to be no he-
roics about it. Persecution was to be wel-
comed as the best of good fortunes. Its
coming was to be hailed with jubilation.

And it must be admitted that the early
Christians entered gloriously into the spirit
of this spirited Beatitude. Caves became
palaces to them, and the wilderness blos-
somed with the rose of Sharon. They sang
in midnight prisons. They wreathed the
lions with garlands of praise. They opened
their arms to the sword. They entered the
flames as a chariot of fire. Starvation was
their meat and drink, and every martyrdom
a mercy. No wonder that the blood of such
martyrs was the seed of a multiplying
church.

No thoughtful Christian of to-day can
read the story of the first three centuries
without asking earnestly: "Has the world
outgrown this Beatitude by its uprightness,
or have Christians become too ignoble for
it? Have we lost the privilege of persecution by indifference and cowardice, and
with it have we lost the promised happiness
of the kingdom of heaven?"

There is no doubt that for "Happy are

the persecuted" we have substituted
"Happy are the popular." We estimate
our statesmen largely by the number of
votes they can get. We value organiza-
tions in proportion to the size of their mem-
bership. Advocates of honorable causes are
obliged to show continually enlarging sta-
tistics. When a man has enemies, when
charges are preferred against him, no matter what charges or by whom preferred, at
once we think less of the man. "No smoke
without some fire," is our charitable prov-
erb.

We are consistent in applying the same
test to our churches and other religious or-
ganizations. We require our pastors to
keep up the number of accessions, and we
count the heads in the pews on Sunday. If
the Sunday schools or the Christian Endeavor societies show a falling-off in numbers, we are eager to supplant them with
contrivances more popular. If the mission-
fields do not report a large number of con-
verts, we question the wisdom of missions.
That false maxim of the business world,
"Nothing succeeds like success," has been
taken over into the religious world, so that
when, from lack of deserved support, a
good cause fails to prosper, it does not
dare to disclose its true condition, but must
wear false diamonds, and ride in a rented
automobile, and run up a bill at the gro-
cer's, in the hope that the show of ac-

complishment may bring the reality in time.

We must not lose the measure of truth that is in the world's Beatitude, "Happy are the popular." "Woe unto you," said Christ, "when all men shall speak well of you!" and yet He prophesied that His crucifixion would draw "all men" to Himself.

It is remarkable how many times our Lord spoke of His glory. It was always in the future, however. He was to come in clouds with glory. It was to be the glory given Him by His Father. He rejoiced that His disciples should behold His glory. Those disciples themselves recognized it even on the earth. "We beheld His glory," John writes. In the first of miracles, that at Cana, we are told that our Lord manifested His glory. While Jesus bade His followers not to love the glory that is of men more than the glory that is of God, He never rebuked them for loving glory.

Indeed, the desire for approval, for popularity, is one of the most deeply seated, powerful, and beneficent qualities planted in us by the All-wise Creator. When the development of our civilization has removed from us the selfish incentive of getting more than our neighbors, the mainspring of progress will be the desire for our neighbors' praise, the approval of man and of God.

This is not an ignoble desire. It has its origin in the purest Christian motive, love and the longing for love. When Christ said, "Happy are ye when men shall hate you," He seemed to run counter to His own plea for universal love.

He seemed to, but it was only in seeming. The two Beatitudes, "Happy are the persecuted" and "Happy are the popular," are one at heart, after all. It is for love that Christians submit to persecution, love of their enemies, whom it would be so much easier and pleasanter to transform into friends by cowardly compliance; and love of God, who died upon the cross rather than curse the world by yielding to it.

I used to know in college a young man whose proud boast it was that he had been driven out of more than one town for his religious opinions. I have forgotten his heresy, but I remember his martyrdom. He was sorely disappointed, I think, that he was not ridden on a rail out of our college community.

But martyrdom is not to be sought. The persecution that makes happy is persecution that is dreaded, not through fear for ourselves, but through fear for others, because we do not want them to espouse the evil and condemn the good. Such persecution leads the world right into the kingdom of hell, though it carries its victims to the kingdom of heaven.

And we pray, Thy kingdom come, on earth as in heaven. Therefore we pray for the popularity of the kingdom of heaven, and of all its glad subjects. Therefore we labor, amid persecutions it may well be, for the end of all persecutions, and for the time when all the world shall become the kingdom of our Lord.

X.

What Is Christian Happiness?

NOW that we have finished our survey of Christ's formula for happiness, what conclusions may we reach?

First, that our Lord sympathizes with His followers' wish to be happy. He is more eager, as we so often say and so seldom believe, to give good things than we to receive them. And it is not a pious pretence of happiness, but the real article, plain, homely, every-day happiness. It does not require a cathedral for its enjoyment. It fits us before we get wings. It attaches itself to us just as we are. It develops us, but we enjoy every step of the process. It is pure gold and not a gold brick.

Second, we may conclude that it is never safe to build our religion upon a single point, upon one idea, one aspect of many-sided truth. A religious structure thus established will soon topple into the ditch of fantastical vagaries, the mire of crankism. All religious extremists, from monks and nuns and hermits and whirling dervishes and holy men stretched upon beds of nails down to Millerites and Dowieites and all other ites that ever founded an -*itis*—every one of these unbalanced fads arose from

[77]

over-emphasis of isolated texts, from a failure to compare spiritual things with spiritual. There is not one of the Beatitudes
but is modified in its interpretation, broad-
ened, deepened, and rendered less paradoxical by association with other sayings of
our Master and other aspects of His character and revelation. If God could not put
all of Himself even into Jesus Christ, but
was greater than the Son, surely He could
not put all of Himself, or even all of His
truth on any subject, into one utterance of
Christ's.

In the third place, we have noticed that
each of Christ's Beatitudes finds a point of
contact with the corresponding, apparently
opposed, Beatitude of the world. The poor
are happy, in spite of their poverty, when
they are poor in spirit; but the rich also
are happy when they are poor in spirit, and
are seeking to make others rich. Mourners
will be happy, and will find a joy denied to
empty-headed laughers; but laughter also
is happiness, when light hearts are laid beneath heavy ones, to lift them. The meek
are happy, and the merciful, and the peacemakers; but these are not happy unless at
the same time they are aggressive and masterful fighters for the kingdom of heaven.
The hungry are happy, but in view of the
time when they shall be satisfied; the pure,
but they may also be experienced; the persecuted, but they are to be the popular.

Fourth, we must remember that every
Beatitude has for its aim, not a continu-
ance of the sad condition in which it starts,
but a purification and glorification of the
corresponding worldly Beatitude. We are
not to remain poor, mourners, hungry, persecuted, but are to become rich, laughing,
satisfied, popular. Our meekness is to be
crowned with the bays of proud achievement. Our mercifulness is to become a con-
comitant of masterfulness. Our purity is
to exist in the largest experiences. Our
peace is to be the issue of heroic strife.
What we need, then, in order to become
truly Christlike, is not to root out our natural emotions and longings, but to allow
Christ to transform them, by the renewing
of our minds, into His likeness. He is to
take the image of the earthy and change it
into the image of the heavenly.

After all, Christ did not need eight Beatitudes to set forth His formula for happiness, but He put it all into a single Beatitude. He said, "If ye know these things,"
—and certainly we do know them,—"happy
are ye if ye do them." The Beatitude is
repeated in the last chapter of the Bible,
"Happy are they that do His commandments, that they may have right to the tree
of life, and may enter in through the gates
into the city."

His commandment is that, however poor
or rich, we shall enrich others, and be rich

ourselves in Him.

His commandment is that, however sad or happy our worldly lot, we shall try to set the world to laughing, and shall rejoice in hope.

His commandment is that we shall be meek for ourselves, but aggressive for Him and His.

His commandment is that, however hungry ourselves, we shall try to satisfy the hunger of the world, and be sure that in the generous activity we shall ourselves find complete satisfaction.

His commandment is that we are to be merciful to the fallen, and masterful to lift them up.

His commandment is that we are to know the sins and miseries of the world, preserving our purity through the purifying of others.

His commandment is that we are so to war against evil that there need be no more war.

His commandment is that we are to endure all persecution while seeking to make Christianity popular.

Happy are they that do His commandments, for they have already eaten of the tree of eternal life, and they are already dwelling in the city of God's love.

www.ingramcontent.com/pod-product-compliance
Lightning Source LLC
Chambersburg PA
CBHW020514030426
42337CB00011B/391